D1212876

abstract art

How to draw and understand it

By GERHARD
GOLLWITZER

STERLING PUBLISHING CO., Inc.   New York

Oak Tr...   ...e Town

OTHER BOOKS BY GERHARD GOLLWITZER

Joy of Drawing

Express Yourself in Drawing

Translated and adapted by Dale Cunningham

Jacket art: Sigrid Senn

Copyright © 1962 by

Sterling Publishing Co., Inc.
419 Fourth Avenue, New York 16, New York

Published in Great Britain by Oak Tree Press, Ltd., London

All rights reserved

Manufactured in the United States of America

Library of Congress Catalog Card No.: 62-18625

Originally published in West Germany © 1961 by Otto Maier Verlag,
under the title *Schule des Sehens*

CONTENTS

An Invitation to Create 5

Rules of the Game 7

Games 1 through 26 . . . . 9 to 84

Color 85

Color Games 27 through 34 . . . . 85 to 101

Color Plates . . . . facing page 88

In Parting 102

Index 107

HE WHO BITES

There

INTO A SINGLE MUSTARD SEED

is nothing

KNOWS MORE

good

ABOUT ITS TASTE

unless

THAN ONE WHO LOOKS

you

AT AN ELEPHANT LOAD

do it!

OF MUSTARD SEEDS.

AN INVITATION TO CREATE

If you agree with the mottoes on the previous page of this little book—the Indian proverb and Erich Kästner's exclamation—you will surely see how true they are in the realm of creative art. For whoever bites into a single seed of art knows more about it than someone who looks at a load of reproductions and reads a load of art books. But at the same time you may ask how to follow this advice in artistic creation. Simply by doing! We shall show you the way. You will develop deeper and happier insight as you play at creating than you could ever obtain by reading books or hearing lectures about art.

We agree with Gerhard Marcks, the German sculptor, who said: "I regard it as a curse that people trust their ears more than their eyes, that they believe what they have read more than what is placed before them. My task, if I may speak so pompously, is to open their eyes."

The goal is to develop your senses and animate your mind's eye, so that you may learn the ABC of a language of pure observation which is indispensable in any genuine artistic training. Our path will not lead up to the great monuments of art *from the outside;* instead we shall trace the growth and transformation of form by playing some games, by doing simple but fundamental procedures. While we are apparently only playing, we are waking, nurturing, and strengthening that intellectual capacity which we all have within us. These games will stimulate flagging imagination, increase the mobility of thinking and acting, and reveal the joy of getting new ideas. This may well have an effect on our whole lives, on the way we cope with and form our lives—in all aspects and forever.

The games all start from certain fundamental creative themes and lead up to personal variations. Although these exercises may seem quite specific, your individual feeling will soon get in tune with them, and you will carry out your own ideas and abstractions in your own particular manner.

We can all follow the same path regardless of talent and previous training, for everyone can create something with meaning. After all, we all begin in the region where the artist and layman are not yet separated, but our activities will help to bridge the present-day gap between the artist and the people, between the artistically creative person and the public which unfortunately looks on inactively, only consumes and enjoys.

The illustrations in the text are not *models* but only *examples*—necessary to supplement and elucidate the text. You will learn to look at the art of all times and cultures as you learn how to create for yourself, and if you desire to continue further than the scope of this book, you will find a few hints at the end of the text.

RULES OF THE GAME

1. To begin with, these are games, not assignments. There is never one single correct solution, but many equally valid interpretations.

Games, not assignments: be completely relaxed yet completely concentrated during the activity; be ready to give every idea free play, but then to form it appropriately.

Games, not assignments: more important than any particular result is your own reaction—what starts and happens in you and with you.

2. Each drawing should be done twice, once standing and once sitting; that is, carried out alternately in large and small formats.

For exercises in a large format use charcoal pencils or charcoal sticks without holders as materials, and simple wrapping paper fastened to the wall or table as a drawing surface.

With small formats, draw with a pencil or a ball-point pen on a writing pad.

3. Pay exact attention to the pointers given for the game. They will stimulate imagination of their own accord, and also keep you from being arbitrary and capricious. When carrying out the pointers, think only in terms of seeing, observing the theme and your variations, and from this finding new possibilities. Abstract concepts need not concern you for the time being.

4. Doing the games with friends is recommended: everyone will start and continue in his own way, but at the end the

many different interpretations should be looked at together, judged, perhaps unified into a greater whole, and each individual will again discover new possibilities for himself.

5. After each game keep your eyes open to note when you meet similar elements of form and methods of execution. You will find them in the well-formed products of human hands, from simple household articles to statues of the gods, from postage stamps to paintings, from peasants' huts to cathedrals. And you encounter them in the immense, inexhaustible, miraculous world of forms and hues in nature.

Beautiful, Mother Nature, is the splendour
Of your invention scattered in the fields;
More beautiful is a happy face
Which thinks the great thought of your creation.
                                        —Friedrich Gottlieb Klopstock

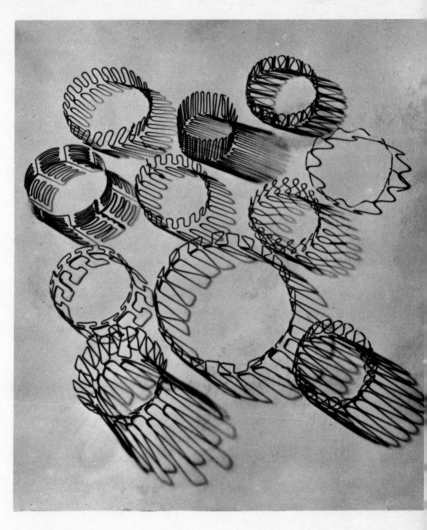

1

If something that can be shaped falls into the hands of a person left to himself, he starts to play with it without thought or intention. At the beach he lets dry sand run through his fingers; he discovers the plasticity of moist sand and is tempted to make forms and build with it.

Given something to make, even people who are primarily practical and profit-minded become childlike. Perhaps we should say they become real human beings again: just as they were when they were children! Another example: *thoughtlessly* our hands make little paper balls out of old theatre tickets in our coat pockets. Let us put the example to the test; put little lumps of plasticine in your guests' hands and then continue the conversation as if nothing had happened. All of a sudden the little lumps will be transformed into little balls or sausages under their fingers.

In just that moment when modern man is *thoughtless*, that is, not thinking consciously, a different, forgotten, almost atrophied thinking stirs: the seeing kind. The basic drive to create form awakes. An urge to order the unordered and chaotic assails him from all sides, an urge to set boundaries for the limitless in order to make things intelligible, comprehensible, capable of being experienced. Even during casual play, *accidental* productions do not arise of *themselves* or *by chance;* no, they have elements of form: balls, ellipsoids, eggs, cylinders—or in sand: circles, straight lines, crosses, lattices, zig-zags, and wavy lines.

2

Take formless lumps of plasticine in your hands one after the other and let your hands play with them until you have several balls and cylinders standing in front of you. The spheres differ from each other solely in size, whereas the cylinders differ in size *and* form, that is, in their different proportions as well.

Now turn your attention first to the balls. These balls are lying on the table. Is this position suitable for them? No, it contradicts their essence, the roundness, the quality of spreading out equally to all sides. They do not want to lie on a support, but to float freely in space like heavenly bodies, or like soap bubbles.

Make your spheres large enough to fill out your hand well. *"Elle remplit bien la main,"* the sculptor Maillol used to say about a good statue. Feel the roundness, tautness, fullness with your hand. A sphere is simultaneously the most exciting and the dullest form: dull and uninteresting because it is so harmonious, complete within itself, objective; exciting because it is so perfect, compelling and concentrated.

3

We will now continue playing with the sphere in two directions. Do not simply deform it, but try to discover what possibilities lie hidden within it.

First let *external force* operate on it. Slap a sphere lying on the table with the palm of your hand or a small board. Drop a sphere on the floor. Turn it over and repeat. Then continue the game more deliberately. Work evenly on each side, as befits the idea of the spherical. You will produce a cube, the angular counterpart of the sphere. However, the more you continue the game, the more closely your product will again approach the spherical.

Next, concentrate the external force at a single point. Push in a little with your finger, then deeper with a pencil, but not beyond the middle of the sphere. Do exactly the same thing on the other side, then halfway between the two, on the opposite side again, and so on. All sorts of problems arise. How deep should the depression be—a very flat dent or a half-round hole? or pointed? and how should the surface appear? blending in without a dividing line? sharply marked? or even with a sculpted emphasis? and what about the number and locations of the holes?

We previously mentioned the macrocosmic spheres, the heavenly bodies. The sphere also plays a significant role in the microcosmos: in the atom and in the seed of organic beings. We all began life as a tiny sphere, and the first step in our development occurred as a small dent which grew deeper and deeper.

4

Inner force! Unfortunately you cannot represent its effect directly; instead, you have to show from the outside what has been caused from the inside. However, you should never forget the basic principle behind this. What are we creating? A single inner force may become an egg, a pear, a drop . . . Two exactly opposite forces may cause an ellipsoid, a double drop . . . Four or six forces? the drawings hint at a few possibilities and problems. What a range there is from a gentle swell or bump to fierce thorns! Clay fruits gather on your table, cherries, apples, pears, chestnuts. And finally you arrive at the converse of the sphere, the star!

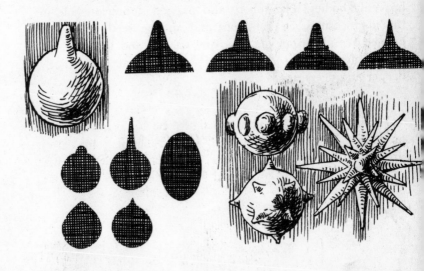

Form a beautiful round sphere once more. Stick it and the star on separate pencils, and devote yourself to studying them. Leave them in front of your eyes for a long time.

Draw a circle. But how? On a large sheet on the table, or better yet on the wall, with your arm stretched out, draw directly from the middle of your body. First circle over the paper like an eagle in air, until gradually your circling becomes visible in a drawn line. Continue circling round and round, farther and farther, until finally—alas!—you have to stop.

This way you have *represented* the circle, abstracted its meaning, realized it as a child does by dancing in a circle. If you had used a compass, you would have merely *constructed* a circle, made a geometric figure.

By the way, how should this figure be understood? First, as itself, a circular line. Second, as the boundary line of an area, a circular disc. Third, as the two-dimensional representation of a three-dimensional form, the sphere.

What does it represent, what does it express? The perfect, the full, the totality, which rests within itself, which is complete within itself without beginning or end, round and right, round and beautiful, warm, soft, protective (the nest!), compelling, forbidding (the magic circle!).

Dante saw the angels circling around God. And God said of the earth's greatest arc, the rainbow, which contains the whole spectrum in itself, "I do set my bow in the cloud, and it shall be for a token of a covenant . . . between me and you and every living creature of all flesh . . ."

"The circling of the stars," Erhart Kästner narrates, "was the greatest nocturnal event. It penetrated us night after night as a doctrine does. This circling of the stars is a show and what happens on earth is only a copy of this and both have only figurative value."

Enrich your circle with itself, with circles within circles, concentric circles. How many, what distance between them? Displace the central points of these concentric circles. Make smaller circles of equal size next to each other, two, three, four . . . intersecting each other, with unequal sizes, irregularly. Then emphasize half of each of the circles and you have a whorl.

Stop for a little while and play with the figure 8 in a circle. Form the outer circle from the left, then both smaller circles, somewhat lighter and greyer than before. Then start with the outside circle again, press more heavily now. Go into the upper circle, across to the lower, and finally return to the outside circle, now in a counter-clockwise direction. The critical point, which you should feel right in the pit of your stomach, is *turning point* (X). In a similar way, you may emerge from an experience you have lived through as a different, transformed person.

Now try to make this symbol without the guiding circles. You will see how much concentration and intensity are needed in order not to get to the bottom too quickly and make it too flat. This is exactly the way we all-too-hurried-people—eager for results—often miss the most important thing.

Now take your most beautiful designs and translate them into three-dimensional forms using strips of ¼-inch wide paper, cutting them into shape, as in the illustration.

Now you may finally construct a circle with a compass. Compare it your your freehand circles: it is exact, but not at all pleasantly so. It is perfect—and dead. In contrast to your growing, living circle—which is always potential and never finished, a symbol of a living community, of an organism, of genuine human living—the constructed circle symbolizes completion, organization, machine manufacture. It contains no element of creative, artistic forming, but represents perfected technology, the artificial. Even its formation is revealing: it originates from a defined point, whereas you do not fix the central point of your freehand circle definitively—even though you do, to be sure, look for it, have an idea of where it is, and circle about it. Place a dot in the middle of a genuinely created circle and it will offend the eye of a sensitive viewer.

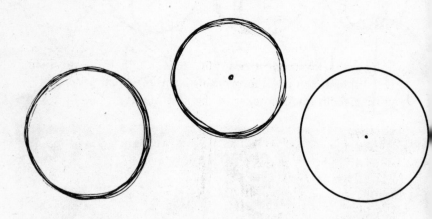

Circles with contrast. Draw straight lines in their most intimate connection inside the circle, through the middle vertical or horizontal. Then draw more pairs. Lo and behold, that mysterious point to which the circle was related, but which was invisible, is now fixed. In fact, emphasis is transferred to it in such a way that the circle loses more and more significance, and we may remove the rim. We have again reached the counterpart of the circle, the star: the beaming, hard, cold object which stretches outwards.

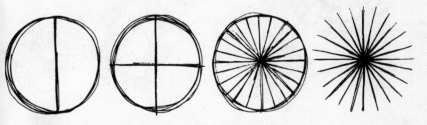

Light beams outward, like a star; our eye gathers in, is round and protective. How else could it be?

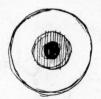
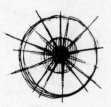

Combinations of the circle and the star.

Connect the beams of the star in various ways to make rectangular areas. Combine these with smaller concentric circles.

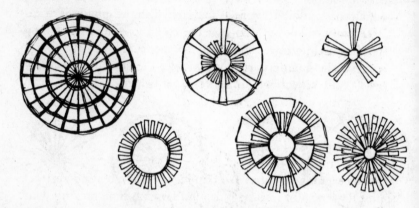

Then represent the star with circles, that is, place circles around a circle in different numbers and sizes. Let the circles play at being stars.

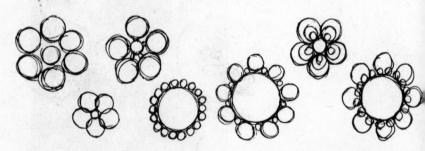

Surround the central circle with the amalgamation of circle and rectangle—the slimmer or more comfortable oval.

Mix all the types in this game and embellish the ends as well.

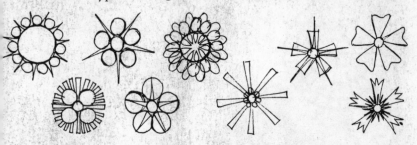

You certainly have noticed that we are now creating abstract buds, flowers, and rosettes of leaves. Lose no time racking your brain for actual examples of botany. Just continue to create variations, for innumerable forms will occur to you.

Cut out squares of grey paper about as big as the palm of your hand. Draw leaf-like rosettes on them, and cut them out. Then cut smaller abstract flowers out of white paper. Paste them all on a large black sheet, distributing them nicely.

Here is a riddle: What does the most intimate union of circle and star look like? It is ʅɐɹıds ɐ! Draw a few—narrow and broad ones, large and small ones.

Shavings from a pocket pencil sharpener.

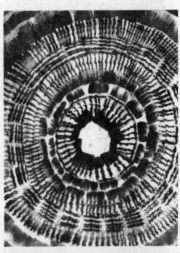

9

Return to the three dimensional again. Cut circular pieces out of tin or other metal foil with the aid of an upturned cup.

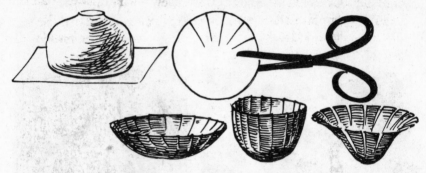

Cut starbeam lines into the disc. Leave a circular core in the middle, and bend up the strips with various curvatures. Begin with very simple forms: cups, half-spheres, and shallow saucers. Then make your cuts at varying intervals and bend the strips up and down alternately—and admire the fairy treasures which collect before you: flowers, lamps, bowls, jewels . . .

Sphere, circle and star—where do you find them in art? In rings, crowns, wheels, in jewels, coins, ceramics, in wood-turning, and basket-weaving, in stone carving, in domes . . .

Perhaps your astonished eyes will be opened anew to "what an endless drama the *pater omnipotens aeternus Deus*—almighty eternal God the Father—spreads out before our eyes." (Paul Cézanne, *On Art*).

"In the heavens the Eternal One sowed His name in glowing stars, but on earth in gentle flowers." (Jean Paul Richter, *Hesperus*).

Look closely at the way beautiful flowers are decorated, at the rich combinations of circles and stars in the umbels of Queen Anne's lace and fool's parsley, of sphere, circle and star

in the stages of development of the dandelion, the thousand little stars of the scarcely valued daisy. Ringlike waves of water, beads of foam . . .

> And if you see a thing you missed,
> Be glad to start all over again.
> —Rainer Maria Rilke

As you have already made the ellipse and ellipsoid in Game 4, now allow further internal and external forces to work on these figures, but this time towards a particular goal, for the ellipsoid and the ellipse are the basic forms of the human face. This should be done in the same fashion as before: *develop* the form from its elements. For that reason, do not attempt to model naturalistically! And do not rack your brains for faces you have seen! To depict a particular true-to-life face would be exactly the opposite of our intention, which is to abstract a face.

Shape several spheres of plasticine with a diameter about the length of two fingerjoints and transform them into ellipsoids. Then continue to vary them: squat, slim, conical with the point up, then down.

Divide the face in half vertically and in thirds horizontally. Mark these divisions with scratches and observe the proportions of the three zones while you are doing this: from the top of the forehead to the eyebrows—to the bottom of the nose —to the chin. Choose completely different proportions for all your heads and try in each case to find the proportions suitable for that head shape.

When you have come this far, imagine that an internal force is pushing outwards from the middle (Game 4!)—that is, put on noses in all possible forms. Now, to your surprise, you will start to recognize many an acquaintance, for the essential thing—which is usually overlooked—has been fixed.

Now you apply external force. To the left and right of the bridge of the nose make two small depressions, the eye sockets. Now the horizontal begins to speak in contrast to the nose vertical. The horizontal also dominates the bottom third, in which you place the mouth. Pay attention to the proportions again: Where is the mouth located? How high?

Finally, give the top and bottom zones—the forehead and the chin—more *character* by making them wider or narrower, by pushing them in or out, and set in the eyes as little spheres.

Do not try to model; continue to do what you did in Games 3 and 4. Again you will discover that you do not run out of ideas, that you do not have to tax your memory at all. Now, with fresh eyes, you will find yourself hunting everywhere for the innumerable variations of the face which in principle is always the same. You will also observe fine nuances as never before.

Return to pencil and paper again. Perhaps you have already tried to draw a face from a live model. "Hold still!" you said. "I want to draw your picture." Then your pencil started stuttering, the erasing began, and both parties got more and more uncomfortable. Finally it may have occurred to you that, after all, the camera was invented for a purpose. How much simpler it is to capture, with a click, a true-to-life picture. Your troublesome quarter-hour of drawing was valuable for you nevertheless. You had probably never observed your model so exactly, even though you may have known him a long time—and this at least was something. But now you must start with a completely different approach, working in exactly the same way as before with the plasticine balls.

Faces from the front form different sorts of ovals. Draw lightly and gently, drawing around the form continuously until it becomes clear of its own accord, and you have mastered it. Draw a whole series one after the other: broad, round, long, pointed at the top or the bottom, triangular. In the process you will recognize, as you did when forming the plasticine, that the form of the face as a whole is crucial to its entire character. Previously, when you tried to draw someone's picture, you may hardly have noticed this because of your impatience to get to the interesting details immediately.

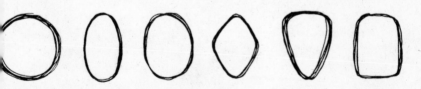

Let us play with the proportions of the three zones of the face. The way they interact on each other becomes clear if you do not draw them into your previous ovals but into a new series of regular ovals, all alike. Instead of a rough, heavy stroke, start very gently. Then you can emphasize the eyebrows a little, slant them up or down, make them diagonal or round them off. The mouth follows next, not plunk in the middle between the point of the nose and the point of the chin, but higher or lower than the midpoint, and in various widths. And last of all, very carefully, the eyes!

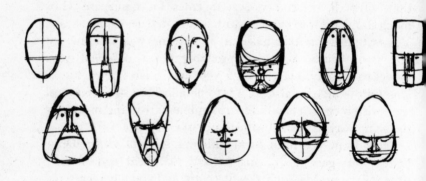

Seen from the side—the profile—the face and cranium of the human head are clearly separated into vertical and round parts. The irregular front contains the four organs—eyes, nose, mouth, and ears. The more regularly shaped rear covers the brain.

Start with a vertical line (for the face) and a circle (1). Then add the neck. Even with this basic form there are differences: some people have an overhanging rear part of the head, and some people have almost no overhang. The next differentiation occurs in the face with its division into three parts and their relationship (2). Finally, faces are set at completely different angles (3).

Start again freely with the basic forms and develop details gradually. Only towards the end should you characterize with the nose, which most people tend to accentuate so much in profiles.

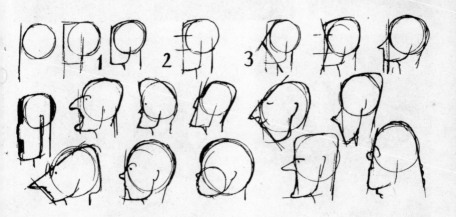

13

Finally give your faces various hairdos. Do not use your previous faces, but draw a new series of similar, regular ovals and a series of similar, regular profiles. Put completely different hairdos on each and be amazed at how they change the faces. Finally, give all the faces suitable hairdos.

Now try cutting out profiles in silhouette—once called the poor man's photograph. Then try sketching profiles in a larger format.

Prints from my own linoleum cuts.

Give the face three dimensions. Pull a sheet of strong white drawing paper about 10″ square over the edge of your table until you create a cylindrical quality. You can get a slimmer or broader basic form according to how pronounced you make the curvature. You can transform it in the direction of the spherical by pulling it in slightly at the top or bottom. Now cut into the paper around the eyes, nose and mouth just far enough so that you can bend the paper up or down and thus create form for each feature. Do not cut out. You are not

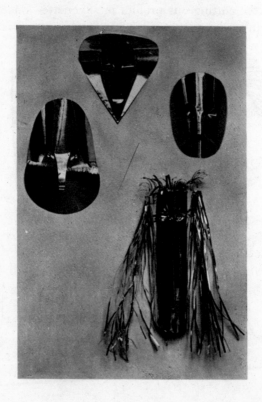

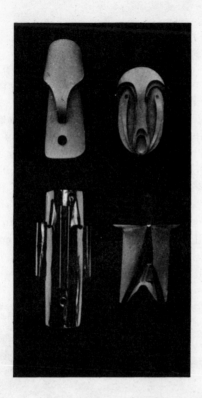

trying to produce a child's mask in short order, but to create characteristic effects with as few means as possible.

Only as a last resort should you paste on new forms, such as curly paper strips for hair. The plainer and more abstract your creation remains, the more the paper as *material* will inspire you, the more ideas will occur to you, and the more expressive your masks will be. Finally, paste a strip across the back to preserve the curvature and act as a hanger.

If you are successful with a few paper masks, it will be fun to repeat them in aluminium foil and to invent new ones in this glistening material. Its brightness accentuates the simplest forms and it retains the curves more readily. There are many modern glues which work on foil.

Before going on to the cylinder, turn your attention for a while to the surfaces of things: to structures and textures. "Adjust" your eyes to such things as the various sorts of paper that pass through your hands in the course of a day. *Look at them and touch them*—your fingertips are just as important for the process as your eyes! Let your fingertips glide over them; the more softly and gently, the more you will feel. Rub the sheets between your fingertips and feel their smoothness or roughness. Extend these experiences to everything you touch: textiles, eggshells, wood, pottery, porcelain, metal . . . Go out-of-doors with this in mind. Look at cement and stone surfaces, the rich carpet of the ground in the woods, the downy,

bristly or scaly quality of animals, tree bark, stone walls, the finish on house walls . . . once you are caught up by this awareness and the rich *cipher writing* strikes your eye, make a collection of such magical things as: glass and pottery fragments, shells, fruit peels, barks, wood shavings from a plane, stones, leaves, metals, textiles . . .

Now create on paper abstract forms representing the textures of all the things you see. Use variously textured pieces of paper about 3″ square and work with all the different materials you can lay your hands on. Do not make designs—instead, let the paper get into tonal or graphic *motion*. Wipe on charcoal, soot, or ink with your finger; dab with your finger or a brush; draw with a pen; splatter; let it flow and surge. Abstract soft downy things, bouncing motifs, lattices, waves, scales, rays . . . Then cut out squares of the best ones and paste your collection on large black or white sheets, mixing in whatever else you can find—sections of photographs or printed paper. As your eyes learn to wander ever more eagerly, and again and again they will stimulate you to make new figures.

Occupy yourself with particular themes: straight lines, either vertical, horizontal, crossing or diagonal; triangles;

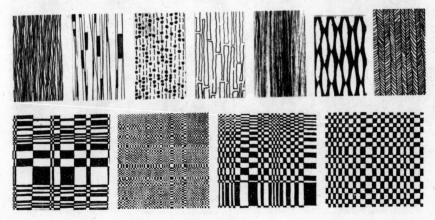

zig-zags or scales. Use all sorts of mediums doing this too and vary your themes in line and tone.

Paste compositions of specimens from your collection onto cardboard. For your first *collages*, cover the entire cardboard. Next, select only a few things which are eloquent in their outline and color and which serve to intensify each other. Arrange them well on a background chosen with consideration.

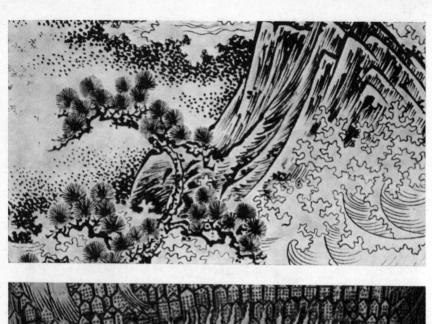

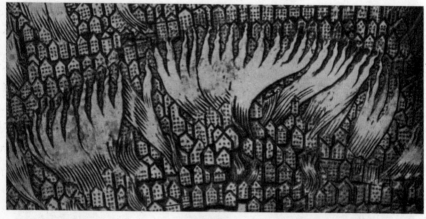

16

We have already encountered the problem of rhythm many times—especially in the last games—without speaking of it explicitly. Let us now turn our attention to it directly. By rhythm we mean an organized succession of movements, a series of similar elements. The rhythm can be regulated or free; the series can be strictly regular or freely swaying—but rhythm always means a living flow. Exact, perfect rhythm is no longer rhythm, but measured time. The time of the metronome or the clock chops flowing time into exact pieces. Living rhythms are the rhythms of our heartbeat and breath, of the seasons and times of day. Put your hand on your heart at night in bed, or your finger on your pulse, and then listen to the ticking of a clock. You will feel the difference. Unfortunately we let our lives be dominated more and more by the measured time of apparatus and motors, of clocks and machines. Rhythm and measured time differ in the same way as do the two circles in Game 6. Genuine, living rhythm is not sloppy, wobbly measure; nor is measured time a perfect, regular rhythm, for they are basically different things.

"In creative art, too, the final, decisive thing in all effect is the rhythm. To be sure, rhythm is nothing else but the heart-beat, and the lack or presence of a heartbeat is a touchstone for distinguishing a constructed piece of work or a work of art." (Ricarda Huch).

After this introductory reflection, let us start to work. Cut a square stamp about as big as your fingernail out of a raw potato. Use the stamp to print stripes on rough absorbent paper. Use thick black ink and vary the succession of stamp and space.

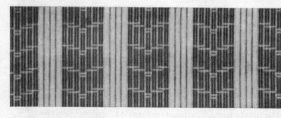

Now use two *voices*—that is, put each two related stripes close together. Then three voices. With each voice the possibilities multiply.

Now try shoving the squares into each other—letting them overlap.

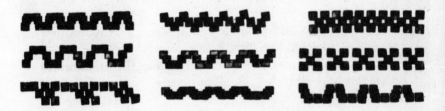

Cut your stamp in half and start over again with the stamp held vertically. Repeat everything holding it horizontally. Mix the two.

Perhaps by now you have noted that there must always be sufficient empty space between the stripes. Your motif should not be too large, for you have to repeat it at least four or five times. Thus you must pay attention to the size of the motif in relation to the width of the sheet.

Soon two types of stripes will result. The first, at rest within itself, is related to a central axis. The second is directed up or down. We shall return to this point later.

Spread your activity out over the entire surface of the paper, first with a square stamp, then a rectangular one, and finally with both at the same time.

Finally, dare to take the step from a regulated rhythm to a free one. Distribute the first prints loosely over the entire surface, and then make an effort to restore the equilibrium which you have disturbed by adding more.

17

For a second rhythmic exercise start with a wavy line. In one stroke, without lifting your pencil, cover your paper with generously swelling curves, small arched curves, waves, figure eights, snake-like lines. Use large sheets of paper, and work standing up. Then use a writing pad, and work sitting down. Repeat this process before every new exercise with wavy lines.

Draw the simplest, most regular curve. This is a new union of the circle, at rest within itself, with the straight line, which surges forward.

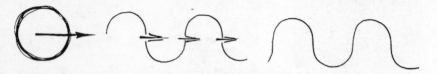

First draw a half circle. Do not let the curve return to its beginning, but continue on to the right. Then another half circle, then to the right again . . . Draw large at first in order to feel the decisive points with your entire body. You already discovered this change-of-direction sensation in Game 6.

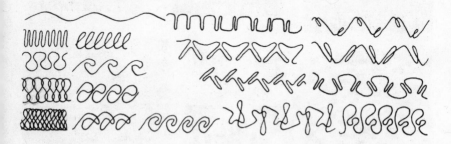

Vary the wavy lines. They can spread out and be wide or narrow and high, surge forward or even curve back on themselves. Now apply to the wave the same rhythmic alternation you just attempted with the potato stamp. Again, pay attention to the size of your motif in relation to the width of the paper.

Let two curving lines play with each other, pursuing each other, reflecting each other, or biting into each other . . . Maintain a regulated rhythm to begin with, repeating wavy motifs.

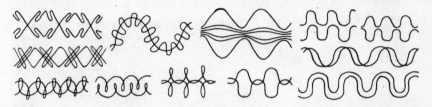

Repeat, larger, with a brush or charcoal. Utilize both light and dark tones.

Now abandon all regulated rhythm. Let the curves play freely and dance in abstract rhythm.

Cover a whole sheet from top to bottom with a succession of curved lines. While drawing, let your mind dwell loosely on an eddy in a stream of water. Next, think vaguely of the grain of wood as you draw. Do not attempt to draw water, or wood,

49

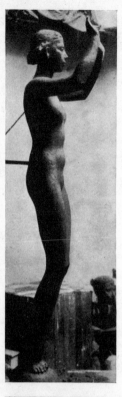

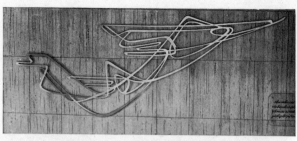

but surrender yourself completely and freely to what occurs to you and to the almost independent efforts of your pencil. Start each time with several horizontals, out of which the movement develops, and work towards the lower edge.

18

Capture wavy lines in a square! Sketching as little as possible in advance, or not at all, cut away curved lines, or *snakes*, from black paper squares about $7'' \times 7''$. Use a razor blade or a pair of scissors. Leave a margin about as wide as your finger to which the snake remains connected. Do not construct snakes in a square; instead, emphasize the contrast between the severe quadrangle and the freely moving curvy line.

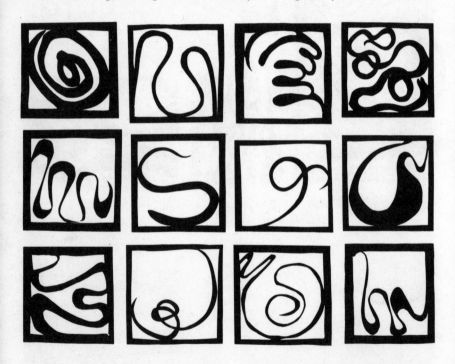

Save the pieces you cut away. Then, using one or more of the pieces, form an abstract composition on an equally large white square.

For the next game you need four large sheets of paper—light grey, grey, dark grey and black, and a sheet of thin tracing paper of the same size. Across the tracing paper draw several free curves which are related to each other—through similarity or contrast. Prepare to trace the best ones by rubbing a soft pencil over the rear of the paper. Turn over the paper again and trace one line on the grey sheet so that the curve touches the top edge, then cut along the line. The second curve goes on the dark grey sheet, the third on the black. The lightest grey sheet remains unused. Now lay the three curved sheets on the light sheet and determine the intervals. The curves may even intersect. If the arrangement pleases you, if the curves play well with each other and if the spaces intensify their interplay, then paste the sheets together and, finally, trim the lower edge. This may not work out satisfactorily on your first few attempts, but soon your eye will feel the harmony and the relationship of abstract curves and tones.

 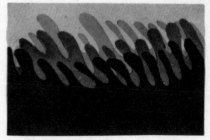

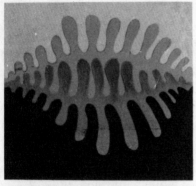

Now let your ten fingers work together at creating similar rhythms and abstractions in wire. Use soft wire about .04″ in diameter. You will soon notice that you need a lot of wire, at

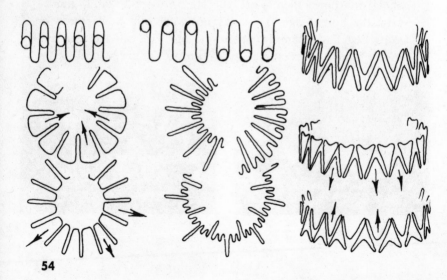

least 20″, for it compresses quickly. After you have created several rhythmic curves, bend them three-dimensionally as well as on a flat surface. Now join the ends of your curved band, first in three dimensions (like a bracelet) and then flat (like a necklace).

The arrows in the drawings call your attention to significance of the different figures at rest within themselves. Some are related to a central axis and others are directed towards one side or another. You can see how architects cope with similar problems in their designs.

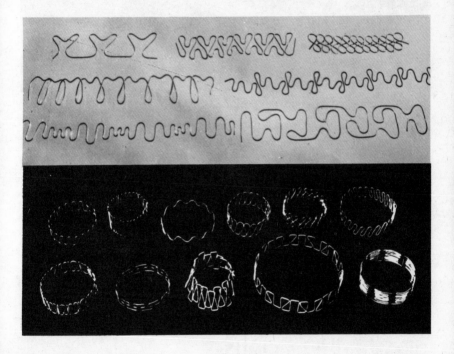

We did not intend to set you up in competition with the jeweler with this last game, but the results certainly indicate a way in which you can use your new knowledge. Looking around again in art and nature, notice that Games 16 through 18 play many practical roles. In architecture, handicrafts and industrial designing, for instance, there are problems in placing windows in a façade, in brick walls, in pavements, in jewelry, in textile design. Consider anew how the curves of hills swing behind each other (18!), how hair curls, how waves or waterfalls ripple, how little streams skip along.

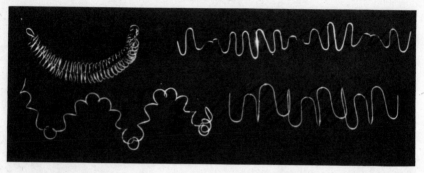

Look at a laurel leaf "with little waves at each leaf's edge like the smile of a wind." (Rainer Maria Rilke).

One more hint: You will find regulated rhythm in the lower forms of life. The higher the form of life, the freer and more exciting is the rhythm in the structure of their forms and in their decorative features.

Work through this game using still another medium—matchsticks. Create the various patterns, pasting the matches on heavy paper or cardboard.

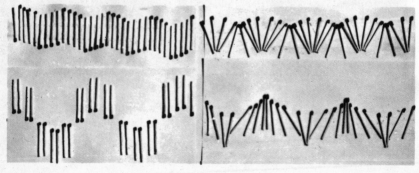

Look back to Game 2. Next to the sphere stands the cylinder. The staff, the straight line and the rectangle belong in its province. Become conscious of this element of form with the most obvious, most elementary means of realization—your body. Sense the tower-like quality of your figure by standing up with your arms hanging loosely, your feet placed slightly apart, and letting your breath escape slowly. Pause and hold

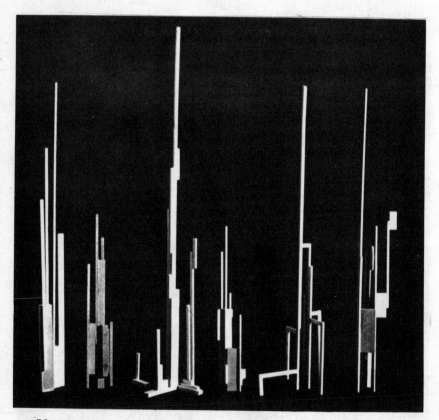

your breath—and when the air rushes in again of its own accord, feel yourself growing up like a tree out of the roots of the soles of your feet. Feel yourself standing there upright like a tower.

Now create abstractions with a tower-like quality in solid form. Use long thin rectangular strips of wood about 1″ or 2″ in cross-section and a strong glue. You have to think in three-dimensional terms, in all directions, and consider your construction from all sides. The multiplicity of even simple forms is revealed when you turn them. Do not attempt complicated models. Instead, carry out a basic theme consistently.

A drawn vertical line can signify either a rising or a sinking— a tower jutting up or a falling drop. Draw a vertical format on a large sheet (newsprint will do) by gliding around its outline without stopping until that which is enclosed by your lines is separated from its environment and the format gets an eloquence of its own. Let the tower ascend within it gradually, towering up out of the broad rectangles of the base to the

Rising verticals

Falling verticals

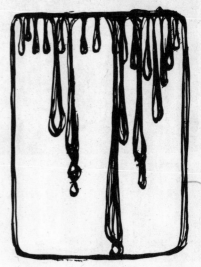

slender point. You have created an abstraction of buildings or whole cities!

Start again with the bordering lines and now let your lines fall from the top and drip down. Pay attention to the composition, to the distribution of the drops, to the spaces between them, to their lengths. Intensify both drawings by using *chiaroscuro*—light and dark tones, or even color. Work with pencil, charcoal, pastels or wax crayons or water colors.

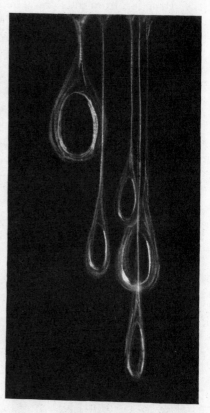

Rising verticals

Falling verticals

Opposite page: Verticals in sculpture and architecture.

20

Make or buy a supply of plasticine cylinders about 8″ high and just thick enough to fit your hand. Now enrich them, using both of the possibilities which a cylinder contains— horizontals and verticals. Scratch point lines onto the surface: few, many, close together, far apart, several in groups.

Deepen or raise these lines three dimensionally, by making troughs and ridges, variously deep and broad. You can create a ridge indirectly by notching the surface. Use a knife to cut your cylinder and study the cross-section.

Another way to enrich cylinders is by means of the other elements they contain: the circle and its relative, the spiral. How can you distribute small or large circles in a cylinder? Continue this game with cylinders made from corrugated cardboard sheets about 6″ × 10″. For inspiration look at cups, columns and towers; look at tree trunks and plant stems! Then paste your cylinders together in various sizes and shapes.

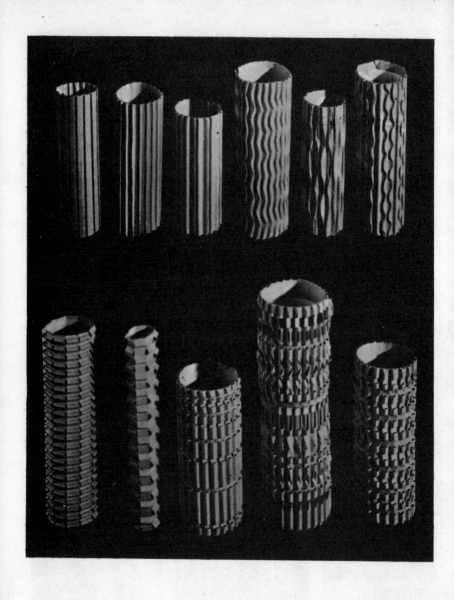

Try creating both variety and unity out of cylinders of different proportions.

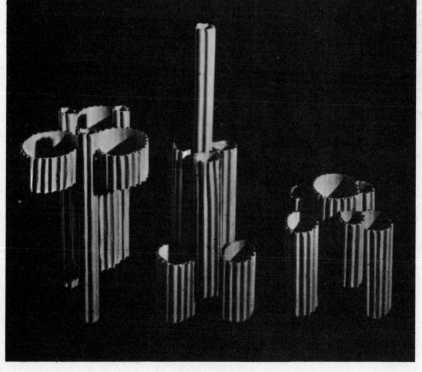

21

Next you will need hollow plasticine cylinders. Make them out of sheets of plasticine which you have pounded flat—about 6" high and 2" in diameter. There they stand on the table in front of you like thick trees. In addition to the strong power within them that drives them upwards, there is also a weaker force that wants to spread out to the sides. The force in the central axis tries to divide itself into smaller forces, multiply, branch out. Begin each drive to the outside from within so that a little bump results on the outside wall. Here—there—where? What relationship do they have to each other? Then continue the driving force, working from the outside. How do the branches continue growing? In which direction?

Where you would have to stop in three dimensions for technical reasons, you can continue for a long time on paper.

Begin to draw again. How is branching out feasible? How do the branches emerge? In what direction? Draw many forms and patterns: opposite each other, alternating, fan-like, straight, curved . . . The farther out the central force spreads, the thinner the branches have to be.

"Trees are the earth's hands." (Felix Timmerman).

Select your favorite results. Now fold various grey and black squares of paper about as broad as the span of your hand. On each folded sheet draw one half of the selected tree. Use simple sketch strokes to serve as a guide for the process of

cutting out, which follows. As you cut, let your scissors create and abstract each tree. Unfold your cutouts—a forest of trees lies before you, helterskelter. Arrange them with deliberation on a large sheet and paste them down lightly. It is not necessary to cover your whole tree with glue.

Now try to make trees in the wind as well.

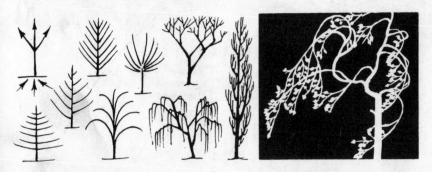

In fall, winter or early spring, you can really feast your eyes on the branches of trees and bushes. How they grasp space with a powerful arm! They stand out as hard silhouettes against the sky or the snow; they emerge as delicate patterns from the fog on dismal mornings.

22

Your fingers are another illustration of branching out. So are birds' claws. But waterfowl have webs between their claws, and in fact the webbed foot of a duck is rather like a leaf. And so we come back to trees! In trees the branching of the structure is continued in the leaves, which are branched-out veins covered by a green surface.

Start to draw leaves about as big as the palm of your hand, beginning with the central axis. Next try various ways of branching out and finally span the flat areas in between. Never begin with the outline or you will be drawing botanically instead of developing creative ideas. Cut out the best leaves and paste them up.

Having prepared yourself to *feel* leaves, go hunting in hedges, bushes and woods. Note your discoveries on your pad and cover it from top to bottom with leaf shapes. Do not copy them timidly, but try to express your feelings about leaves and clusters of leaf shapes by means of symbols for them. At home you can start again, this time composing and abstracting more deliberately.

71

23

Now that the last exercises have led us out into nature, let us stay there! To be sure, we do not intend to copy a landscape in all its detail with pencil or brush. Far from it! We are going to look at it from one particular aspect, trying to learn to see the whole. To do this we must first investigate the relationship of things to each other and learn to find the main element. Among the objects that at first appear to be of equal value, we will seek to find the particular form-theme to which the secondary themes and individual details are subordinated.

Prepare yourself for this at home. Draw various rectangles— large and small, low horizontal formats, comfortably solid and narrow slender vertical formats, and squares at rest within themselves.

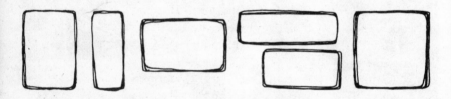

At first you will work only with these two elements, the horizontals and verticals. Begin each time by outlining the border as you have done before and then, without lifting your pencil from the paper, enter the outlined area. Place a few vertical lines, then several. Next try horizontal lines and then both together in the rectangles. Do not work abruptly or mechanically. Even a single line changes the feeling, and of course each additional line changes it still more. At first draw your lines across the entire width or the entire height so that later, when you make them shorter, you will continue the feeling of flow-in-the-air.

While you are doing these seemingly simple exercises, keep thinking of vague landscape motifs, of the horizon at sea, of a lake with reeds, of a forest interior with slender trunks, of a lonely pine on a hill with horizontally moving clouds . . . Without effort, you will express these abstract ideas in your drawings.

Beginning again with the outlined formats, add slanted, diagonal lines at various angles and in all sorts of ways. Keenly observe their relationship to the horizontal-vertical border and be aware of the way they influence the picture area. Draw diagonals and parallels to the diagonals, and then lines at right angles to the diagonals. Finally, having considered the problem thoroughly, start with a few slanted lines and then accentuate their feeling with more slanted lines. Remember always to feel your work in your entire body. Standing vertically, from time to time during the day, let your mind or body concentrate on the vertical.

If you have been carefully observing and analyzing your results, you should by now be impressed with the completely different moods which result from the stability of horizontal or

vertical lines and the dynamic quality of the diagonals. Now, if you have been working loosely, not stiffly as in a geometry exercise; with feeling, not merely mechanically; and if, finally, the circle and the curve are still alive in your mind and eyes even as you arrange the horizontals, verticals and diagonals— then you are well prepared to combine them all in the excursions that follow.

Go out of doors without drawing materials and let your eyes search, discover, and sweep about actively. The horizontal surface of the lake will call to you there, and so will the curves of the mountain beyond its banks, the verticals in the reeds, horizontals and diagonals of all kinds—a telephone pole, a board, a boat—the stripes of the fields moving against each other on broadly swaying hills—the tree spheres distributed in a loose rhythm in a field or at the edge of a hill—a house as a single, horizontal-vertical block at rest amid the dynamic diagonals—the pine tree triangles jutting up high on black forest slopes . . .

Consider what you see not as objects but as abstract themes. Think about architects, and how they abstract the themes of nature in the buildings they design. Gradually your fingers will start to itch. Next time, take your sketchbook along.

When you start drawing out-of-doors a new problem awaits you, what to include on your sheet! Where should you stop at the right and the left, top and bottom? When I was young there was a seductively tempting implement for overcoming such problems: little black frames called viewfinders. That is not what you need or want, for your object is not to chop a view out of landscape but, on the contrary, to concentrate the whole broad abundance into a picture. Therefore, do not begin by searching for a view—find a theme that entices you, and only then ask yourself—with your outstretched hand held vertically and horizontally—how far you want to stretch the frame and what format you want for your theme. In fact, make the experiment of fitting the same theme to several formats.

To be sure, once you start to draw you have to start in reverse, beginning with the format of the finished product.

Decide where to locate the theme, and fit it into the picture area with horizontals and verticals. You must determine, too, how large to make the most important object or critical space. Once you have fixed this dimension, it will determine all the other proportions as well.

Now draw in the other lines which mark important directions. Make them quite long—completely or almost completely

across the surface of the picture—in order to train yourself to see and discover *relationships*. That, after all, is the object of your activity. Next draw whatever is revealed to your eyes in such relationships. Let your eyes do your thinking for you!

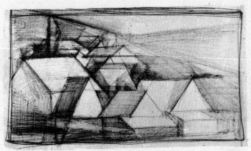

Enrich your line drawing with *chiaroscuro*—contrasts of light and dark. Try many different means, such as cross-hatching with your pen; pen drawing with a *wash*—tones painted in with brush and thinned India ink or color; soft pencil, whereby you simply wipe in the tones with your finger; or for larger formats, use charcoal without a holder.

Two hints: Do not be tempted to start out by toning too dark. You do not want to bring up your heavy artillery prematurely. And do not fill in complete areas; instead, as you proceed away from the theme, simply add a tonal area to this or that edge. This will force you to pay even closer attention to the relationships of things to each other.

Once again look over all the exercises you have done up to now. You will discover many a compositional or rhythmic deficiency—and even mistakes. Do them over again now, with your increased understanding, and see what progress

you have made. After all, the object of your activity was not
so much the particular result but enriching and opening up
your mind and soul, waking up your slumbering visual power
to understand and produce art.

26

Do you know that every day, without thinking about it, you use the elements of linear form? Seldom does a day go by when you do not write something, and our writing, developed from the Roman alphabet, uses characters composed of horizontals, verticals, diagonals, and circles. The very letters we use are abstractions of pictographs and hieroglyphics used in ancient times.

Draw lines about 2″ to 3″ apart on white paper and between them draw Roman letters. First compose the letters made of verticals and horizontals, then those with diagonals, and finally those with circles and half circles. Even at this stage you have to give much consideration to proportions. You must consider not only the relation of the width of each letter to its height, but also estimate the amount of space each letter takes up.

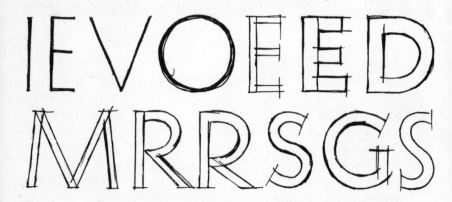

Cut the letters out and paste them on dark sheets as words or as chains of figures. Stand them in lines or distribute them freely over the sheet or place them close together or loosely scattered. When you do this, forget their usual purpose as strokes symbolic of conceptual thought. Discover their artistic quality. And pay attention to the spaces in between!

The game becomes even more exciting if you use tinted paper as well as white, and if you intertwine the letters as well as placing them next to each other.

Now draw the letters as thin lines and enrich them by enlarging them in various ways and by making the stops (top, bottom, and at the sides) artistic—that is, give them form. Start with the simple letters—the I and the O. Try making the alphabet hard and angular, then start again with softness in mind and gentle transitions. Perhaps you never thought there was any art involved in the type for a book. From the few examples given here you can see how the choice of type influences the character of a book.

Compose monograms of letters of the same type and of different sizes and styles. Merge them so that the two letters become one. Work out your most successful results in a larger size and more carefully.

IIIIE ABGRS
GWWW MEMPHIS
ABCDEPQRS BERLIN
PROSPERO FIDELIO

Our final game stimulates a final thought. If you now look at the many sorts of handwriting and consider that they are all nothing else but variations on a single original alphabet, then it begins to dawn on you that the vast symbolic writing of art and nature, this overwhelming abundance of forms, has not been created by arbitrarily stringing up senseless fragments of form one after the other, but by consistently carrying out variations and amalgamations of only a few elements of form in an artistically logical way and according to rules. What a drama then unfolds before our eyes—a play, not an idle pastime without rules; a play infinitely full of fantasy yet not fantastic; a play with basic themes that can be surveyed and comprehended yet with a rich abundance that is immense and overwhelming.

COLOR

The activities concerning color do not lead into a new and separate segment of art. Color belongs to *all* areas. Actually we see only colors and spots of color in nature and in art. The hours which you devote to color should belong exclusively to color. Attempt to be conscious of its particular essence and its particular values. Even during the final, most advanced games, try to pay attention only to color.

27

Collect all sorts of tinted paper from wrapping paper to the insides of envelopes. Cut out a lot of small squares about the size of a thumbnail and spread them out before you. Begin the game by arranging this profusion of colors, sorting the pieces according to their relation to a few main colors: yellow, red, blue, green, and white-black-grey. Even this sorting will pose problems for you. Many little squares will wander from the green pile to the blue, or even from the blue to the red and back again, until you finally have to put them between two color groups. Now on separate sheets of white paper paste up a small mosaic selection from each pile. Paste the little bits close together with no white gaps between them!

What differences are apparent when you look at your sheets?

Can you think of any more bases for the arrangement of your colors? How about separating the light and dark bits of paper within each color group? And then grading them according to the degree of lightness? You can also differentiate between the clear and muddy colors, arranging them according to their degree of purity. Next try arranging them according to intensity, power, or saturation.

Imagine the world of color as a globe. At the North Pole is pure white—"every-color" which contains all colors. At the opposite pole is black—the absence of color. The axis, therefore, represents pure grey from the lightest to the darkest. The pure primary colors—red, yellow and blue—and all the

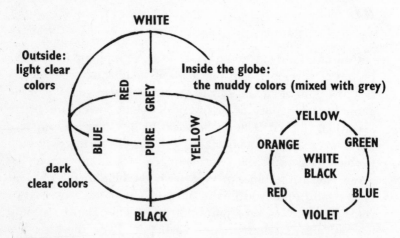

transitions between them, are arranged on the surface around the equator. Now you have proved that green, which you may previously have thought of as a separate color, is a mixture. All the pure light colors are in the northern hemisphere of the globe, all the pure dark colors in the southern hemisphere. The interior of the sphere contains the murky or dirty colors (mixed with grey or black). The closer to the axis, the murkier are the colors.

Study your mosaic sheets again. What a number of variations of each color! And still you have only a small selection of all the possibilities. But you have made the first and most important step in your color education. From distinguishing between different colors you have progressed to an understanding of each color. You no longer merely differentiate between blue and red and yellow, but between blue and blue. On the top one-third of your yellow, blue and red mosaic sheets, outline each little paper square with heavy black lines. Now observe what happens to the areas of color: the differences between shades of each color speak out more clearly, the tension between the colors is intensified. On the rest of the sheet, however, the colors tend to merge. The little squares have a more modulated, less vivid effect. Observe the effect of the black fillets in stained glass windows. The black dividing lines intensify the power of the translucent stained glass.

28

Look again at your grey sheet. Now you can see more clearly that it contains little pure grey, but rather that it is much more of a reddish, greenish or bluish grey. Actually, you encounter pure black, white and grey less often than you think.

Make up another set of similar mosaics, leaving room for heavy white separation lines, and observe their effect.

The more sensitively your eyes begin to react to the finer differences in color, the more you will like grey. "No one is a painter until he has painted grey," said the great color expert Cézanne.

For the next game you need a fairly large supply of light grey squares. Divide the pile in two so that each half contains exactly the same shades. Each of the two sheets you are now going to prepare should contain the same colors, with no particular shade to be found on only *one* of the sheets. Using one pile, arrange the little grey squares of paper into a mosaic on a fresh sheet of paper. For this part of the exercise, try to avoid all contrast. Aim for a soft, cloud-like effect, gradually progressing from light to dark, from bluish grey to reddish grey, so that the separate little squares can hardly be seen any more from a short distance.

With the second pile, on the contrary, you will try to emphasize the contrasts—light-dark contrasts as well as color contrasts. Make it as vivid as possible. Try, as you work, to give the abstract idea of a clown's patched costume with these mildly tinted squares. If you show both these sheets to someone not in on the game, he will hardly believe that they each contain the same tones.

Repeat the game with medium grey squares.

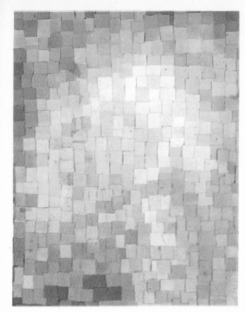

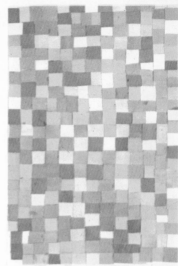

See page 88

See page 88

See pages 89-93

See pages 89-93

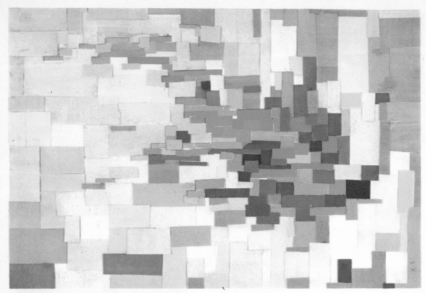

See pages 91-93

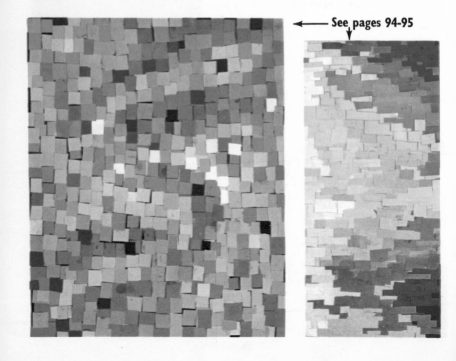

See pages 94-95

See pages 96-99

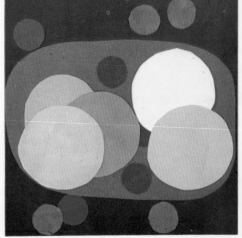

See pages 98-99

29

The last game showed how sensitive colors are, and how dependent they are on each other and on their surroundings. Only the strongest of all retain their character; most of them react to every change in their surroundings. One could almost say that color does not exist, it happens—happens when it associates with other colors.

Spread large sheets of colored paper before you—strong ones and restrained ones, brilliant ones and muddy. Have an equal number of smaller sheets, all of the same grey. Place a grey sheet on each colored sheet and look closely at the surprising results. It is hard to believe that the small sheets were all cut from the same piece! The degree of lightness seems entirely different on the white background than on the black. The more delicate the grey you use, the more noticeable the influence of the background color becomes. You will get the most striking differences of all if you use light greyish violet. On which background is the effect most intense?

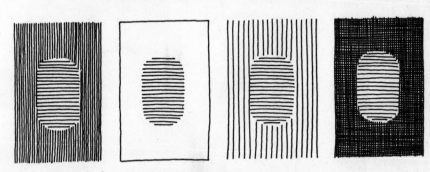

Do the same thing with stripes. Cut strips of equal width from a sheet of colored paper and paste them at intervals of the same width on sheets of very different colors.

Investigate this interplay of color wherever you are and wherever you go. Consider the natural objects you find along your path and when possible play with them just as you did previously with the little bits of colored paper.

For example, a stone which shimmers like opal tempts you. You pick it up and take it home. If you put it on a white tablecloth, its magic disappears! What color background will make it glisten again? Take out the collection you made for Game 15 and you will see it with completely new eyes. It will stimulate you to play such games as this.

30

Colors are influenced by light as well as by one another. Not only do they intensify and subdue each other, but our search for contrast also leads us to still another aspect of arranging colors, the contrast between warm and cold. What is meant by that? Warm: imagine fire, a flaming glow. Cold: imagine the sky on a clear, frosty winter morning.

Hunt out warm bits of color from your supply for one pile, and cool bits for another. Place the two groups next to each other on a dark grey sheet. Can you describe the different effects in words? The warm group is active and seems to spring forward. The cold, on the other hand, is passive; it recedes. The effect becomes even more striking if you paste warm papers around a cold axis. Then put the warmest of all, the most glowing, at the very heart of the axis. After this try the opposite. Place cold colors around a warm center, with the coldest of all for the bull's-eye.

 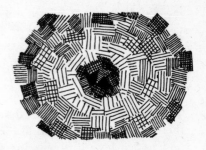

The warm-cold contrast reveals the dynamics of color clearly. and introduces a third dimension to our surface activity. Paste up the warmest reds and the coldest blue-green bits in checkerboard fashion, and the flat surface appears to be a *relief*—to have high and low planes. A room with a light blue ceiling appears higher; one with dark red, lower. Mural painters of the baroque period made liberal use of this effect to heighten domes.

The papers you have collected will no longer supply your needs for our next games. You will have to color some for yourself. Use opaque water colors—you will need a set with six or twelve colors along with a tube of tempera white—or, preferably, use all tempera colors. Buy the cheapest and smallest tubes of white, black, cadmium yellow light, yellow ocher, vermilion, madder lake, cobalt blue, ultramarine, English red, burnt umber, and chrome green. You also need one or two flat hair brushes about $\frac{1}{4}''$ and $\frac{1}{2}''$ wide, and a palette or a pane of glass.

Press out the tempera colors neatly along the edge, leaving sufficient room for mixing. Stir the color to a paste (not too watery), mix it well, then apply it to cover completely. Do not mix the paints in their holders or in the little heaps pressed out on your palette. Paint with the point of the brush and always have a cloth at hand to dry out and clean your brush. Always clean your brushes, for palette and water colors become thoroughly set right after you stop working!

Paint only by daylight. Mixing colors is an exciting affair. Many a color is so intense that even a tiny addition of it is enough to change the mixture completely. White makes colors colder as well as lighter: for instance, warm English red immediately changes to cold pink with the addition of white.

Tempera color is the dullest, most sober opaque, and therefore the most suitable for our games. Look around you and notice how different the same color appears in different materials. For example, compare the same red in dull tempera, in transparent watercolor, in glistening oil (oil color permits all the nuances from a thick, pasty application to a thin glaze), in glass, enamel, wool, silk, velvet, stone, ceramic glaze, or wall paint.

Create an abstract picture in the warm-cold theme. Imagine

92

a fire burning in the snow on a winter morning! Work out the theme as a mosaic, this time with rectangular slips of various sizes. Choose all sorts of reds from fiery glowing reds to somewhat cooler ones. You will also need cold blues and greys.

Warms and colds, however, are not limited to these two colors. You can find this contrast within each hue itself. There is a warm blue—ultramarine—and a cold blue—cobalt blue. There are warmer and colder reds, yellows and greens, although the spread is least in yellow. Mixtures of red and blue are ambiguous and therefore are especially sensitive to their surroundings. You have already used the warm degrees of red in the last mosaic; now paste up a blue mosaic sheet for the warm-cold theme. Your bits of paper can be square or rectangular, but utilize the whole scale from blue-green to violet. Think of fish swimming around in the cool depths of the ocean, as you work. Or perhaps you prefer to think of snow-covered mountain peaks. Do not try to compose a fish, or the mountains, but merely try to express their feeling abstractly.

31

The previous games made you conscious of the most intense color contrast. Some colors, on the other hand, negate each other. Have you ever noticed, for instance, that certain stripes of equal width placed next to each other look like an over-all grey from a little distance? Which ones are these? They are the ones which are exactly opposite each other on the color equator—the complementary colors. When mixed with each other, they result in grey.

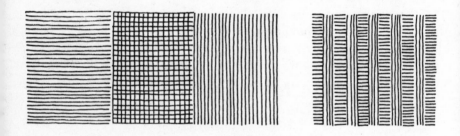

Paint an area as big as your hand with any color at all. Leave a little of the paint mixed on your palette for the moment. Now try to work up the exact complementary color in exactly the same degree of lightness, and paint an area with it just as big as the first. Then mix equal amounts of the two remainders of paint together. If your colors were truly complementary, the resulting mixture will be grey.

Cut narrow stripes from one of the painted areas and paste them on the other one at intervals as wide as the stripes. Hang this sheet on the wall. It flickers when you look at it close up, but the farther you go away from it, the more the stripes disappear into a shimmering grey. In contrast to the tendency of the warm and cold colors to disrupt the surface area, the complementary colors enjoy merging. They hold the surface area together. Cézanne applied these effects most effectively in his famous watercolors.

Here are two magic tricks:

Lay small bits of medium grey on sheets of various strongly colored papers and cover them all with white tissue paper. The grey now looks completely different. It appears to be the complementary color of the background.

Lay a strongly colored 2″ square on a light grey background. Stare at it a long time and then take the color away quickly. A spot of the same size in the exact complementary color will appear in its place.

32

Now let us try one more mosaic stressing the contrast between clear and muddy colors. Using many nuances of a single murky color, paste up small squares on a sheet. If necessary you can paint a sheet with little rectangles. You now know how to muddy or grey colors—that is, to make them approach the grey axis—by mixing them with their complementary colors. Now paste on or paste in a few completely pure spots of the same color so that they glow like jewels. From the dominance of the few pure specks of color over the many murky colors you discover still another aspect of arranging colors: the intensity of pure color.

Repeat the same game with stripes of color.

33

Advance now to more complicated mosaic compositions, combining everything you have learned about color so far. It is too soon to expect to paint masterpieces. There is a long road ahead of you before that. However, you can approach that end, even at this stage. By *painting* color compositions in mosaic, as you have been doing, you avoid the risk of insipidly *coloring in drawings* instead of *creating with color*.

Try the following exercises with square or rectangular bits of paper. Think about your subject as you play with the pieces. Then distribute them approximately—many greens down below, a straggle of coral-colored squares for the snake, etc. Move them around, arrange and rearrange them, feel your subject, before you paste them down.

A green snake among the leaves.

A city by the river on a bright sunny morning.

A city by the river in the evening.

A city by the river in a dismal mood.

For the last three themes try using larger rectangles as well. In addition, you may want to use diagonals to give the effect of sloping hills between the abstract sky and houses. Do not try to be explicit, though. Remember that your themes are meant only to suggest objects, to stimulate your imagination to be the means to a particular goal in color.

Create an abstract still life with circular cut-outs. A bowl of fruit is your subject. Select a harmonious concordance of color and paste up a circular fruit bowl and many large and small circular fruits.

You can do these exercises simultaneously in an even more abstract fashion—using stripes alone. On a second sheet of paper paste the same colors in different widths corresponding to their density in the other pictures.

Find still further themes for yourself, such as flowers in a meadow, clouds, stormy skies and so forth. Paste up these compositions, varying your basis for arranging colors. Remember to go back and repeat in colors the games you performed in greys in Game 28.

34

Are you ready to paint for a change? Use a brush, then, but guard against mere coloring-in of drawings. Select a motif but do not paint forms. Just make patches of color with a flat brush and without a preliminary sketch. Start from the spot that interests you most and put down patch after patch. Do not paint one object or form completely. Instead, continue working from the first patches of color in every direction—into the middle of the object, then out into the background. Paint easily from part to part without thinking of the composition of the picture. You are really trying to develop a keen *ear* for the language of color. Your final result should look rather like a hooked rug, not a realistic drawing with the perspective worked out by means of chiaroscuro—light-and-dark effects. If you have been successful in working with color and not colored drawings, the important part of your painting would disappear in a black-and-white photograph.

You will find it helpful to start with toned paper. Color your paper first with a neutral color applied with a brush and lots of water and then wiped with a cloth. On this background even the first patches will stand out more vividly. In order to avoid garishness choose objects related in color, such as a group of fruits in the yellow range: lemons, oranges, bananas—whole as well as cut open and peeled. Place them on a bright background—a yellowed board or a used paint rag. Put your still life on a stool in broad daylight, lighted from the front, so that you can look at it from above.

At the same time paint your motif in stripes on another sheet, just as you previously pasted up the color composition of your picture in stripes. In fact, start with a striped sheet and then lay it aside. Study your motif and then paint it in the broad patches of color described above. After a few hours—if possible, dedicate a whole day to this work—comes a second striped sheet, not taken from your picture but from the motif! Put it aside, continue studying and painting and end the day with a third striped sheet. Now take out the others and compare all three. If you have worked and concentrated successfully, your last efforts will be richer and more varied, and at the same time more unified.

When the paint is dry, place your final picture flat on a table. Take four white sheets of paper and slide them over it from each side, searching out the most successful parts. Perhaps the lemon is too loud—cover up enough of it so that just the right amount of its sharp yellow remains to kindle the other colors. If the grey of the background is too muddy, eliminate most of it. Perhaps you will need to add a speck of orange to liven it up and make it appear colorful. Mark the best sections with a pencil and cut them out.

If you should succeed in painting a complete picture as good as one of your final segments, with nothing which needed to be eliminated, you would be a good artist! As you know, an artist needs a large measure of experience, and the effort of a lifetime. Artists strive all their lives to see and master the relationships of forms and colors, to learn and control their language. You have already made a modest but genuine approach and now share a bit in their concerns and activities. You will now observe their works with more understanding. As you view art of all sorts—abstract or otherwise—you will understand what the artist is aiming at and what he is trying to convey.

Remember too that painting pictures is only one of the many activities in the extensive realm of creative art. From time immemorial only a few people have devoted themselves to it exclusively, even in the ages when art was still an important concern in the lives of many people. But today, as always, the opportunities to exercise your growing awareness of color, form, harmony, and so on, exist constantly in simple everyday pursuits. May your newly animated powers of seeing prove themselves more and more often—first on modest occasions, such as a festively set table, a harmonious tie, shirt and jacket combination; or the considered choice of carpets, curtains, or materials for your apartment. May your architectonic education reveal itself in arranging furniture and hanging pictures, your understanding of graphic art in a card of congratulations or an invitation that you have thought out yourself.

Linoleum cut by Frederike Wetzel.

Hand etching by Max Hunziker from Grimmelshausen's *Simplicimus Simplicissimus*.

And whenever you go out into nature now, you will notice how much your capability of experiencing things has expanded and deepened. No longer merely enjoying with the emotions, no longer merely observing with the natural scientist's eye, but seeing and looking, you will now absorb an abundance of forms and understand them in a new way. The works of artists will increase your understanding of nature, and your new understanding of natural forms will enable you to view art, especially abstract art, with a new feeling of enlightenment.

In Parting

On the most moving day of her life, when she is left alone in the tower chamber, Hero says:

> They also put a lyre in here.
> I never learned to play it,
> but I wish I had! Thoughts
> crossing my brain, chaotic and wild,
> would dissolve more easily in tones.
> —Franz Grillparzer,
> *The Waves of the Sea and of Love*

Or in colors, forms, or lines. Being able to express ourselves through an art form not only dissolves our tensions more easily but enables us to cope more fruitfully with our daily experiences. Even what is disconcerting and incomprehensible we can judge and evaluate and assimilate better, and make a deeper part of ourselves.

> When God's world becomes
> invisible through the window's frost,
> grief grows more hopeless,
> more and more like the desolation
> of the high seas.
> —Boris Pasternak

Let us not allow frost to gather on the windows of our soul and our minds, but let our eyes learn to see with comprehension. Our games have started the process for you. Keep it up! The secret of life is hidden in the forms of nature, yet manifest and capable of being seen. Beyond the visible reality lies the true, invisible reality which creates it. For, the most noble human sense of all is seeing.

My linoleum cuts for Melville's *The Noble Rooster Beneventano.*

ART WORK PICTURE CREDITS

The photographs of art other than my own used in this book to illustrate various concepts are:

The sphere, circle and star—on page 11 a photograph of *Soap Bubbles* by Franz Härle; on page 12 *Restless*, made of straws by Gudrun Esterl in 1958; on page 23 detail from *Noli me tangere* by an anonymous North German master at the beginning of the 15th century, now in the State Picture Gallery, Stuttgart; on page 26 *Stupa 2* built about the last half of the 2nd century B.C. about halfway up the hill at Sanchi, India; on page 28 the rose window in the west façade of Strasbourg Cathedral built about A.D. 1270, and *Buddha in abhaya—mudra*, a sandstone statue of the 5th century A.D., now in the Indian National Museum, Delhi.

The Face of Man on page 34—a Greek grave offering of 2000 B.C., now in The Louvre, Paris; *Head of Christ*, a wood carving of about A.D. 1070, now in St. George Church, Cologne; *Güstrow Memorial*, a bronze head by Ernst Barlach in 1927, now in Antoniter Church, Cologne; *Head of a Woman*, a wood carving by Ewald Mataré in 1925; *Hans Purrmann*, a bronze head by Emy Roeder in 1950; detail from *Mother and Child*, a bronze by Gerhard Marcks in 1957; *Indian Woman*, a bronze by Helmut Ammann in 1957; detail from *Self-Portrait*, a lithograph by Käthe Kollwitz in 1941.

Textures on page 42—detail from *Hero at the Sea's Edge*, a pen and ink drawing by Hokusai in 1816; detail from *Cologne in Flames, 1945*, a bronze door of Cologne Cathedral, by Ewald Mataré; detail from *Krishna and Radha*, an 18th century A.D. miniature of the Kangra School, now in the Government Museum, Madras, India.

Strict rhythm (left) and flowing rhythm (right) on page 44—(top left) an Italic-Etruscan gold filigree bracelet of the 7th century B.C., now in Munich; (top right) a bracelet by Nele Bode about 1950; *Stephansdom* of about 1400 A.D., Vienna; a choir screen of 1743 in Abbey Church, Amorbach, Germany; drapery fabric by Alice Lund of Sweden about 1955; *abstracta-plastic* (a plastic sheet) of the Göppingen Calico and Artificial Leather Works, Göppingen, Germany; the parapet of a restaurant, by Bengt Gate, 1955, Hälsingborg, Sweden; script sculpted in stone.

Curved lines on page 50—*Grave Monument*, a bronze by Hermann Haller about 1925; *Winds at Play*, a wall decoration by the author in 1958; detail from *Adam and Eve*, an engraving by Albrecht Dürer in A.D. 1504; detail from *Waves*, wood cut from *Mangwa* by Hokusai about 1820; detail from *Peach Trees by a River* by Ogata Kôrin, now in Shizuoka-Ken Atami Museum.

Verticals (top) and the profile of the cylinder (bottom) on page 61—*Apollo from Tenea*, a marble statue of the first half of the 6th century B.C., now in Munich; the spire of a 14th century cathedral, Freiburg in Breisgau, Germany; *Campanile* (bell tower) by Giotto and Andrea Pisano in the early 14th century for the cathedral in Florence, Italy; early 14th century columns in the cathedral in Wells, England; *The Chariot Driver from Delphi*, a bronze of about 470 B.C., now in the Delphi Museum, Greece.

Enriching cylinders on page 63—porcelain vases by Sven Erik Skawonsius of

Denmark about 1950; a Frankish drinking cup made of glass of the 7th or 8th century, now in the Museum of Pre-History and Early History, Berlin; a glass with nobs of the 15th century, now in the Museum of Art and History, Hamburg; a Chinese porcelain jar; the tower of an old fortress; 13th century compound columns of the cathedral in Cologne; inside a cathedral of A.D. 1290 in Vienna.

Composition and landscape on page 80 including—*Monk by the Sea*, a painting by Caspar David Friedrich in 1809; *Summer*, a painting by Claude Monet in 1874, now in the State Picture Gallery, Stuttgart; *Trees by the Water*, a watercolor by Paul Cézanne about 1900, now in the E.M. Remarque Collection, Ascona, Germany; *Mountains in Spring* by Kao Jan-hui about A.D. 1275-1300, now in the Count Sakai Collection, Tokyo.

ABSTRACT ART

INDEX

Axis, 46

Background, color, 89, 90
Balls, 11, 12, 29
Botany, 23
Buildings, 60

Camera, 31
Cézanne, Paul, 27, 88
Character, 30
Charcoal, 7, 49
Chiaroscuro, 78
Circle, 16–27
Colors, 85–87, 89, 97
Compass, 19
Contrast, color, 91, 94
Crayons, 60
Curves, 17, 56
Cylinders, 62–66

Dante, 17

Ellipse, 29
Ellipsoid, 15, 29
Equilibrium, 46
External force, 13, 29, 30

Face, 33
Figure 8, the, 18
Figures, 69
Fingertips, 38

Form, elements of, 10, 58
Formats, 7

Grillparzer, 102

Hairdos, 35
Handwriting, 84
Head, human, 33
Hero, 102
Hesperus, 27
Huch, Ricarda, 43

Inner force, 15. See also Internal
    force
Internal force, 29

Kästner, Erich, 5, 17
Klopstock, Friedrich Gottlieb, 8

Landscapes, 72
Leaves, 69, 70
Letters, 82
Light, 21

Maillot, 12
Marcks, Gerhard, 5
Masks, 37
Monograms, 83
Mosaics, 85, 93, 95, 96
Motif, 46, 98

Ovals, 22, 31, 32

Painting, 98
Pastels, 60
Pasternak, Boris, 102
Plasticine, 11, 62
Profile, 33

Rectangles, 22, 72
Relationships, 77
Relief, 91
Rhythm, 43, 48, 49, 54
Richter, Jean Paul, 27
Rilke, Rainer Maria, 28, 56

Silhouette, 35
Spheres. *See* Balls

Spirals, 25
Stained glass, 87
Stamps, 43, 45
Stars, 21, 62

Textures, 39
Themes, 76, 92, 97
Three-dimensional forms, 19, 26, 36
Tones, 53
Trees, 67
Turning point, 19

Water colors, 60, 92
Waves of the Sea of Love, The, 102
Wavy line. *See* Curves